中英双语版

企鹅经典 名人大发现

艾萨克·牛顿

［美］珍妮特·B. 帕斯卡尔（Janet B.Pascal）◎著 ［美］蒂姆·福利（Tim Foley）◎绘 杨琼琼◎译

Who Was Isaac Newton?

湖南科学技术出版社 小博集

·长沙·

著作权合同登记号：字18-2024-199

图书在版编目（CIP）数据

名人大发现. 艾萨克·牛顿 ：汉英对照 /（美）珍妮特·B. 帕斯卡尔（Janet B. Pascal）著 ；杨琼琼译，（美）蒂姆·福利（Tim Foley）绘. -- 长沙 ：湖南科学技术出版社，2025. 1. --（企鹅经典）. -- ISBN 978-7-5710-3265-4

Ⅰ. H319. 4

中国国家版本馆CIP数据核字第2024A8Y553号

上架建议：科普读物

QI'E JINGDIAN · MINGREN DA FAXIAN：ZHONG-YING SHUANGYU BAN AISAKE NIUDUN

企鹅经典 · 名人大发现：中英双语版　艾萨克 · 牛顿

著　　者：[美] 珍妮特 · B. 帕斯卡尔（Janet B. Pascal）
绘　　者：[美] 蒂姆 · 福利（Tim Foley）
译　　者：杨琼琼
出 版 人：潘晓山
责任编辑：刘　竞
策划出品：李　炜　张苗苗　文赛峰
策划编辑：马　瑄
特约编辑：杜佳美
营销编辑：付　佳　杨　朔　周晓茜
装帧设计：利　锐
内文排版：金锋工作室
出　　版：湖南科学技术出版社
（湖南省长沙市芙蓉中路416号　邮编：410008）
网　　址：www.hnstp.com
印　　刷：三河市航远印刷有限公司
经　　销：新华书店
开　　本：875 mm × 1230 mm 1/32
字　　数：103千字
印　　张：5.125
版　　次：2025年1月第1版
印　　次：2025年1月第1次印刷
书　　号：ISBN 978-7-5710-3265-4
定　　价：22.00元

若有质量问题，请致电质量监督电话：010-59096394　　团购电话：010-59320018

目录

Contents

谁是艾萨克·牛顿？

1665 年，一种可怕的疾病在英国蔓延，这种疾病叫瘟疫。患有这种疾病的人会全身肿胀，皮肤变黑，没有任何治疗方法。大多数感染的人都会很快在痛苦中死去。而且瘟疫具有传染性，任何有人群集聚的地方都很危险。

没有人知道病源是什么，也没有人知道怎么做才不会被感染。唯一安全的办法是到乡下去，那儿人少，不容易感染瘟疫。

此时，二十三岁的艾萨克·牛顿还是一个学生，他不得不离开剑桥大学逃往母亲的农场。他对瘟疫一点也不关心，因为他一直是个独来独往的人，也没有值得想念的朋友。在母亲的农场生活的那段时间，他一直在思考他擅长的领域——宇宙。

一天，牛顿看到一个苹果从树上掉落下来，便开始思考是什么把苹果拉向地面的。因此，根据这个著名的传奇故事（可能确有其事），年轻的艾萨克·牛顿想到了万有引力。

对大多数人来说，瘟疫蔓延的那些年真的糟糕透了，但是对牛顿来说，并非如此。对他来说，那是一段充满发现的美妙时光，他不仅发现了万有引力，还有了很多新想法。而这些新想法足以让他余生忙于思考和写作。他的想法帮助人们以一种全新的方式去理解宇宙的运转。

十八个月后，牛顿回到了剑桥大学，但他始终没有交几个朋友。他忌妒心强，对人也不算友好，还很容易发脾气。他也许不是一个很好的人，但却是世界上最伟大的科学天才之一。

艾萨克 · 牛顿

第一章

孤独男孩

艾萨克·牛顿生于 1642 年的圣诞节，出生地是英国林肯郡。（由于当时英国使用不同的计时日历法，他的生日也被记录为 1643 年 1 月 4 日。）

一开始，他的未来似乎不被看好，甚至他似乎都不会有未来。他是个早产儿，身体虚弱，小得可以放进一个容量仅为一升的杯子里。没有人认为这个病弱的婴儿会活下来，但是他活下来了。他的父亲也叫艾萨克，在他出生前三个月就去世了。他的父亲在世时，是个特别富裕的农民，但是不会读书和写字，甚至都不会写自己的名字。

艾萨克三岁时，他的母亲汉娜再婚了，嫁给了一个名叫巴纳巴斯·史密斯的教士。史密斯想要的是一个妻子，而不是一个儿子。汉娜答应搬到丈夫的新家生活，而把艾萨克安排到了外公外婆家。

英国内战

牛顿刚好出生在英国内战开始的时候。在他的童年时期，英国国王和议会陷入了残酷的战争。1649 年，也就是牛顿六岁的时候，英国国王查理一世被判绞刑死亡，一个没有国王的严格政府掌权了。十一年后，即 1660 年，查理二世恢复了君主制。虽然牛顿的家人没有被卷入战争中，但这种时代的暴动性和不确定性对他的童年造成了巨大影响。

此后，小艾萨克几乎没有再见过他的母亲，他感觉特别孤独。有时，他会爬到树上凝视着母亲的新家。他憎恨他的继父，脑子里想过要在继父在家时一把火烧毁他的房子。然而，艾萨克十岁时，他的继父去世了。

他的母亲又搬回了外公外婆家，同时给他带回来了一个同母异父的弟弟和两个同母异父的妹妹。

艾萨克去了当地的乡村小学读书，除了识字，学校里也没教什么了。他看起来特别聪明，因此汉娜决定送他去更好的学校就读。七英里[①]外，有一所国王学校，走

① 英美制长度单位，1 英里 = 5280 英尺 = 1.6093 千米。

路上学距离太远，所以艾萨克就在镇上的克拉克家里住。克拉克家的人后来回忆说，艾萨克住在他们家时，爱上了他们家的女儿凯瑟琳。如果确有其事，凯瑟琳就是他唯一有过的女朋友。

多年后，凯瑟琳回忆说："牛顿是一个头脑清醒、沉默寡言、喜爱思考的少年。"她从未看过他和其他男孩出去傻乎乎地玩。他学习之余，会制作娃娃家具送给凯瑟琳。

克拉克是位药剂师。药剂师是将草药和化学药品混合在一起制造药物的人。这种工作对称重和测量的过程需要十分小心，还要清楚不同物质的特别之处。小艾萨克对此十分着迷。通过观察和帮助克拉克称重和测量，

他开始学习基础的化学知识——不同物质混合在一起时是如何互相作用的。他甚至会自己调配新药剂，比如用松节油、玫瑰水、蜂蜡、橄榄油、一种叫麻袋的葡萄酒和红檀香配制的药剂——这种新药剂可以保护他，不受一种叫肺结核的致命疾病的侵袭。

艾萨克还对记录时间的方法十分着迷。当时记录一天时间的时钟不是很精确，所以他想改良一下时钟。后来，他绘制了从日出到日落的影子变化轨迹图。然后，他在墙上钉上木钉，制作了一个日晷。当人们想知道准确的时间时，就会去看“艾萨克的日晷刻度盘”。为了让

人们在室内也能看到时间，艾萨克设计了一种木质表盘时钟，由持续滴落的水提供动力。他还发明了一种小风车，由一只老鼠带动。

不幸的是，艾萨克对学校的课程不感兴趣。他不学习，成绩在班里垫底。一天，一个成绩好的学生踢到了他的肚子，艾萨克立刻向对方发起挑战，让所有人惊讶的是，他赢了。然而，艾萨克是个胜负欲极强的人，只是打赢了架，对他来说还不够，他还想在学业上打败他的对手。因此，他开始努力学习。很快，他的成绩就上升到了班级前列。

学校开设的主要课程是拉丁语和希腊语。这两种语言对他以后的学习很有帮助，因为当时几乎所有重要的书和文章都是用拉丁语和希腊语写的。他可能还学过一些简单实用的算术课程和几何学课程。

汉娜以为，接受教育主要是教她儿子成为一个好农夫。不久后，她觉得是时候让儿子经营农场了。于是，她把儿子从学校带回了家。然而，艾萨克觉得种庄稼和照看动物的活特别烦人，所以，他故意不好好干农场的活。

要干农活时，牛顿就会坐在树篱下读书或做东西。有一次，牛顿本该看守羊群，但他却让羊群闯进邻居的田地里吃庄稼。

因为这件事情，牛顿的母亲被告上法庭，还被罚了款。因此，艾萨克根本就没有如他母亲所愿，成长为他母亲希望他成为的那种农夫。

第二章

就读剑桥

幸运的是，并不只有艾萨克一个人讨厌他当农夫。他学校的校长认为，做农夫会浪费聪明的大脑。校长和艾萨克的舅舅一起成功说服了汉娜，让她的儿子上了大学。于是，在艾萨克·牛顿十八岁时，母亲送他去了剑桥三一学院就读。三一学院是剑桥大学的一个学院，接下来的四十年里，艾萨克就住在剑桥大学，起初是一个学生，后来成了一名教授。

在剑桥大学的最初几个月里，牛顿感到特别失望。尽管汉娜家境富裕，但是她并不想支付艾萨克的学费。因此，牛顿不得不以减费生的身份入学，这就意味着，他要为更富裕的学生提供服务来挣学费。

这里的大多数学生更热衷于享乐，而不是学习。牛

顿鄙视那样的学生。后来，他遇到了另一个和他一样学习认真的同学约翰·威金斯，从此他不再那么孤独了。他们搬到了一起，并一起生活了二十年。威金斯是牛顿为数不多的有着长久友谊的朋友。然而，不幸的是，威金斯一生中，从未写下他对牛顿的回忆。

牛顿在剑桥的学习依然以古希腊和拉丁哲学为基础，尤其是希腊哲学家亚里士多德的作品。亚里士多德是一个杰出的人——可谓是他那个时代的牛顿——但是他却是公元前 4 世纪的人。然而，两千年过去了，各个领域的知识还是保留原样，没有任何变化。

亚里士多德

亚里士多德的种种理论基于他对周围世界的观察，他认为，一个合情合理的观点更重要。然而，他并不总

剑桥大学

牛顿所处的那个时期，很少有人真正去上大学。英格兰只有两所大学：牛津大学和剑桥大学。两所大学都十分古老，它们的主要目的是将学生培养为英格兰的牧师。因此，只有教会成员才能上大学，每个学生都有一个负责教育的个人导师。然而，对很多上层阶层的学生来说，上大学的目的只不过是享受美好时光而已。

是依据现实来验证自己的想法。比如，他认为男性比女性更加高大、强壮，所以男性比女性拥有更多的牙齿。这样的观点对他来说，合情合理。要是他真正观察过男性和女性的口腔，就会发现他的这个观点是错误的。在他去世后的数个世纪里，其他学者通常只是把亚里士多德的观点奉为真理。

牛顿对剑桥大学的许多课程并不感兴趣，他也很少关注这些课程，他在意的是剑桥大学藏书丰富的图书馆。

过去的几个世纪里，一些有胆识的学者对有关世界如何运转的古老方式的解释的质疑从未停止。当时还没有科学家这个词——人们称这样的学者为自然哲学家，他们是现代科学的奠基者，是牛顿学习的榜样。

牛顿阅读了尼古拉·哥白尼的观点和理论，他是一位质疑亚里士多德理论的学者。亚里士多德认为，地球是宇宙的中心，也是围绕地球转动的所有天体的中心。16 世纪的哥白尼认为，地球和所有其他行星围绕太阳转动。牛顿认为哥白尼的观点似乎合情合理。

尼古拉·哥白尼

亚里士多德的观点看上去好像是对的——对我们来说，似乎所有的东西都是围绕地球转动的。但是任何真正观测过宇宙中行星运行的人都会发现，行星的运转方式和亚里士多德描述的情况有时并不相同。

人们提出了各种复杂的观点，来解释行星为什么没有像亚里士多德描述的那样运行。但是，如果人们不再强迫自己接受亚里士多德的行星运行观点，转而接受哥白尼的观点——所有行星围着太阳跑，一切就会变得明朗起来。行星真的就如哥白尼学说预测的那样运行着。

亚里士多德的观点

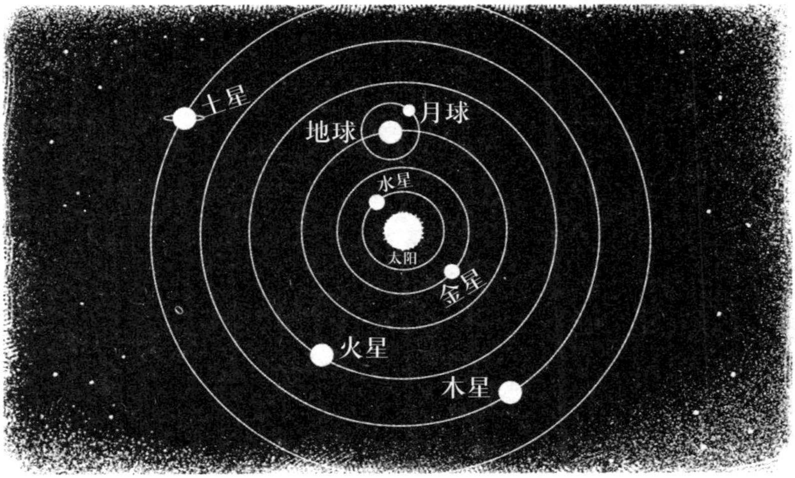

哥白尼学说

牛顿还阅读过约翰尼斯·开普勒的著作，开普勒的理论是在哥白尼理论的基础上建立起来的。

约翰尼斯·开普勒

哥白尼认为，行星是绕着太阳运行的，运行轨迹是圆形的。开普勒仔细追踪了行星运行轨迹，最终发现了

行星运行的真实轨迹：行星运行轨迹并不是圆形的，而是数学上称为椭圆形的一种轨迹。

伽利略

在牛顿出生的那一年，意大利天文学家伽利略去世了。他曾用望远镜观察天空，并报告了令人惊讶的发现。比如，月球的表面布满了山脉和陨石坑，太阳上都是斑点。然而，亚里士多德认为，天体一定是纯粹的，比地球上的任何事物都更完美。伽利略的观察发现表明，他持有和亚里士多德不同的观点。他认为，即使是遥远的月球，也是由和地球上一样普通的物质组成的。

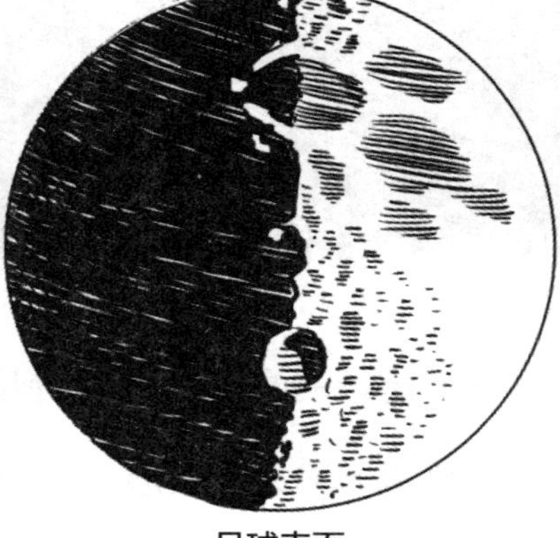
月球表面

伽利略认为，其他人的观点要通过测试证实一下，才能确定是否属实。比如，亚里士多德认为，重物比轻物下降速度更快。这种观点听起来很有道理，但是伽利略却想知道真实情况是否如此。于是，他想了个实验，把球从高处丢下去，然后测量球下降的速度。传说伽利略是从比萨斜塔上把球丢下去的，其实，真实情况并非如此。但是，伽利略的那次实验，却证实了亚里士多德的观点是错误的。从相同的高度丢下相同大小和形状的物体，不管物体有多重，或有多轻，它们的下落速度是相同的。

阅读了这些伟人的著作后，牛顿有了一些体会。他领悟到，一个观点听起来多么合情合理其实并不重要，重要的是它必须与实际观察到的相符。如果这个世界和现有观点描述的不一致，那么就到了要提出新观点的时候了。

牛顿在剑桥时就开始自学数学。这一兴趣源于斯陶尔布里奇市集，他去了一次市集，这是一个巨大的户外市集，很多农场农夫和商人在那里卖农场牲畜、衣服和玩具。市集热闹拥挤，有年轻夫妇，有舞蹈家，还有动物表演，比牛顿通常喜欢的地方要“轻浮”得多。然而，他在那里看到了一个书商，并买了一本有关占星术的书。

占星术是一种信仰——认为星星和星球统领着人的生活。占星家们用天象预测未来，并试图控制地球上发生的一切。占星术在那个时候发展得异常复杂，需要用图表进行复杂的计算。

在牛顿生活的时代，很多人相信占星术，他也对此感到好奇。阅读这本新书时，牛顿遇到了一个他不懂的数学难题。因此，他买了另一本书进行自学。但是为了理解这本新书，牛顿不得不去学习一个他还没有学习过的更加基础的数学分支知识。因此，他不得不从头学习基础知识。

1665 年，牛顿通过了种种考试，获得了学士学位。

他的学业成绩并不是很好，因为他对大多数考试题目测试的有关知识不感兴趣。尽管如此，他的成绩也足以让他获得学士学位。这就意味着他能继续在剑桥生活和读书，享受免费的食宿。然而，就在他获得继续留在剑桥的资格时，他又迫不得已离开了剑桥。

第三章

瘟疫那些年

1665 年，英国暴发瘟疫，大学停学，牛顿回到了林肯郡的家中。

接下来的十八个月的时间里，他一直住在家里。牛顿向来不太喜欢与他人相处。能够单独留在家里，牛顿对此感到很开心，他刚好能好好思考自己想要什么，这段时间成了牛顿人生中成就最多的时期。他后来回忆道："那段时间，我正处于发现和创造的黄金时期。"他所说的发现是指发现新观点。

牛顿发现了什么新观点呢？首先，他在数学上有了新发现。已知的数学知识能够帮助他很好地解决一些问题——如果人们知道一辆马车的行驶速度，也知道马车的行驶轨迹是圆，那样很容易就能算出这辆马车一个小时后会到达什么地方。然而，牛顿却对另一个不同于此的问题感兴趣——他想知道一直在变化的事物。如果人们发射一枚炮弹，会发生什么呢？首先，炮弹会沿曲线轨迹向上飞行，然后速度越来越慢。当炮弹到达轨迹的最高点时，它就会沿着曲线轨迹重新返回地面。炮弹越来越靠近地面，速度也越来越快。炮弹的速度和方向一直在发生变化。如何能够创造一种数学方程式，来描述这种速度和方向一直在变化的运动呢？

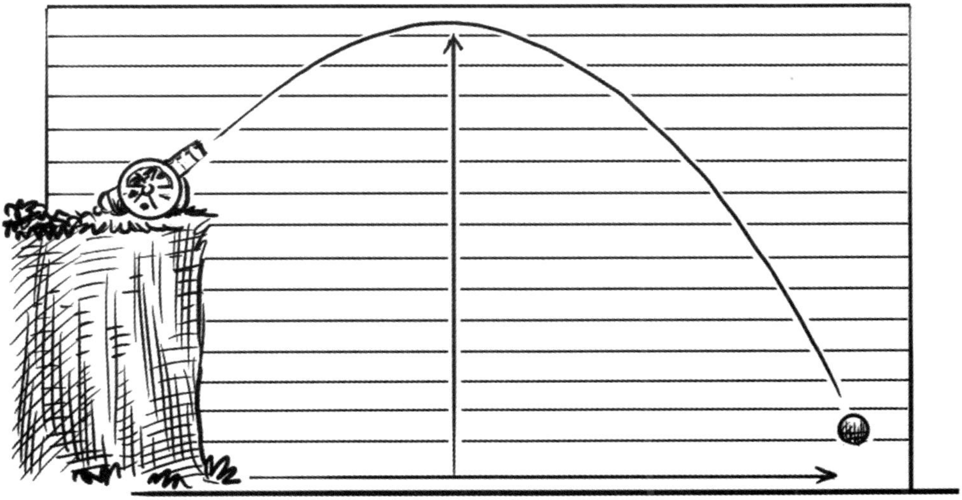

英国瘟疫和伦敦大火

瘟疫肆虐时，伦敦成了一座死亡之城，约有五分之一的人死于瘟疫。然而，到了1666年9月，也就是瘟疫逐渐平息的时候，伦敦发生了一场大火。这场大火开始于一家面包店，大火蔓延了三天。大部分人都设法逃离了伦敦，但是伦敦百分之八十的建筑物都被烧毁了。尽管当时没有人知道，瘟疫是由老鼠和跳蚤传播的。这场大火烧毁了老鼠居住的肮脏的旧建筑，这可能对瘟疫的消失助了一臂之力。

牛顿自己发明了一种算法——一种可以解决以上问题的方法。他称之为流数法①，流动的意思是“持续变化”。我们今天称之为微积分，没有微积分，就不会有研究运动、物质和能量的现代物理学。

牛顿一直感兴趣的另一门课题是光学。他在斯陶尔布里奇市集买了一个棱镜，这是一块形状奇怪的玻璃。光线穿过它，就变成了一道彩虹（我们称之为光谱）。牛顿开始摆弄这个棱镜，检验他先前学到的关于光的知识。

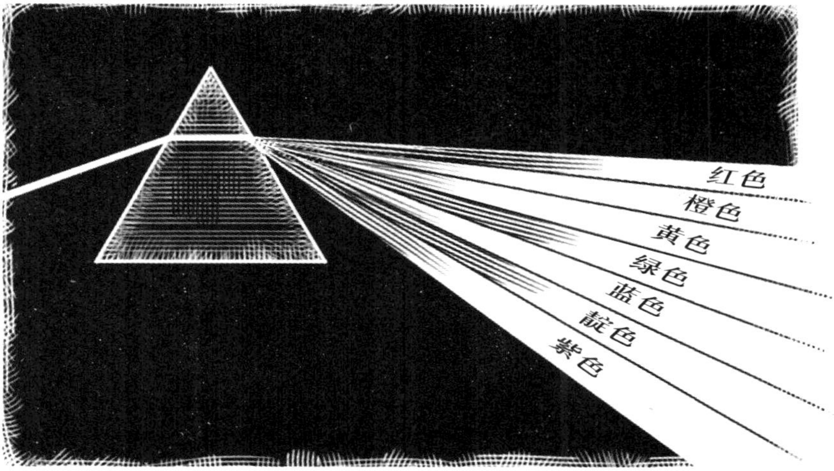

① 流数法（method of fluxions），fluxion 意为流动。

亚里士多德认为，光的基本形式是纯白色的。其他颜色都是白光变化形成的。如果给白光一点变化，就有可能看到红光。再给白光一点变化，就可以看到橙光，以此类推，就得到了所有颜色的光。但是，牛顿现在已经知道了，亚里士多德有时是错误的，他对光的认识就可能是错误的。

牛顿清楚知道，白光穿过棱镜时会分解成光谱上各种颜色的光。如果让那些发散的光谱色光再次穿过棱镜，会发生什么呢？如果白光穿过棱镜变成了各种颜色，那么第二次穿过棱镜的光应该会发生更大的变化。然而，事实上，光没有发生更大的变化，而是在第二次穿过棱镜后，重新组合在一起，又形成了一束白光。

这一现象让牛顿想到了其他问题。如果让一种颜色的光再次穿过棱镜会发生什么呢？他做了一个实验去查明真相。首先，他让一道白光穿过一个棱镜，形成了完整的光谱。然后，他留下光谱上的绿光，让其第二次穿过棱镜。如果亚里士多德说得对，第一次穿过棱镜的白光已经发生了变化，变成了绿光。绿光穿过棱镜时会怎么样呢？绿光会再次变成完整光谱的颜色的光吗？还是只是发生一点变化，变成蓝光？相反，牛顿发现，第二次穿过棱镜的绿光没有发生任何变化，绿光穿过棱镜后依然是绿光。

牛顿的实验证明，亚里士多德的说法是错误的。白光并不是光的基本形式，相反，白光是各种不同颜色光汇聚在一起形成的光。棱镜并没有改变白光，只是将白光分散了，使之分离成了不同的部分。

牛顿对光的发现解开了一个谜。除了牛顿，没有人能解释天空中为什么会出现彩虹。牛顿意识到，空气中的水滴就像棱镜，把太阳的白光分散成了红、橙、黄、绿、蓝、靛和紫几种颜色的光。他能够解释，白光穿过自然界众多棱镜后，是如何形成彩虹的。

第四章

坠地苹果

牛顿在母亲家里的那一年被称为他的“annus mirabilis”，这个拉丁语的意思是奇迹年。一个年轻人能够在这么短的时间里弄明白这么多问题，简直是一个奇迹。发现光的真正属性和发明微积分只是个开始，牛顿随后又开始致力于研究以他名字命名的运动定律和万有引力理论。这个著名的故事讲述了牛顿是如何通过观察坠地苹果而发现万有引力的。而且，这个故事很可能是真的。在晚年，牛顿自己也说过，他最初的万有引力的概念是“由一个苹果的掉落引起的”，而伍尔索普庄园内的确种了苹果树。

亚里士多德认为，东西坠地是因为重物有自然向下坠的本能趋势。牛顿觉得亚里士多德的说法又错了——认为重物有向下坠地的本能趋势是没有道理的。他认为，一定是存在一种什么力量把东西拉向地面。

如果真的存在这种力量，那这种力量到底有多大呢？牛顿相信，这种力量可能是无穷大的。把苹果拉向地面的力量也可以作用于月球和行星。

这是一种令人惊讶的全新观点。在牛顿所处的时代，人们认为，宇宙中存在两种力量，一种是地球上的力量，另一种是月球以外的力量，这两种力量截然不同。因为人不能到外太空去，因此没有办法研究。这就意味着，没有人能了解宇宙在人们能到达的那一小部分之外是如何运行的。

现在，牛顿心里早已确定，如果研究苹果的坠落，他

就能知道那些作用于宇宙中的任何事物上的力量。他越想这件事情就越确定，那种让苹果从树上掉落的力量，正是那种使月球围绕地球转

动，而不飞向太空的力量。

没有人确切知道，牛顿在他的奇迹年中对这些想法研究得有多深入，也没有人知道他后来又弄清楚了多少。过了很长时间，牛顿才跟人们分享了他的这些想法。

牛顿一生都讨厌公开他的发现。只有当他非常肯定每个细节都做得非常完美的时候，他才会向其他人公开自己的发现。无疑的是，牛顿不想让任何人发现，他的想法可能是错的，他似乎还喜欢独占自己那些大胆而又令人激动的想法。

第五章

妙不可言的望远镜

1667 年，瘟疫结束了，牛顿重返剑桥大学。他的一个老师鼓励他向世界公开至少一个他的发现。这个老师名字叫艾萨克 · 巴罗，他是当时剑桥大学第一名数学教授。

艾萨克 · 巴罗

1669 年，牛顿给巴罗教授看了一篇他写的有关流数法的文章。看到牛顿使用的数学新工具，巴罗教授感到十分惊讶。他认为，牛顿发明的这个工具太重要了，不应该只是他一个人知道。牛顿这才勉强同意巴罗教授把他的文章给一小部分人看，但是他还是很坚定地拒绝发表这篇文章。

1669 年 10 月，巴罗教授离开了剑桥大学。他高度认可牛顿，因此，他安排牛顿接替他担任数学教授。多亏了巴罗教授，牛顿终于过上了他真正想要的那种生活。他不需要花太多的时间和精力去完成他的职责，他所有的工作就是讲几堂课。他的课乏味难懂，几乎没有人去听。

牛顿根本不在乎这些，他对那些学生或教授根本不感兴趣。他大部分的时间都穿着不合身的衣服，披散着银色的长发，在大学校园里闲逛。

牛顿经常忙于思考而忘了吃饭。剑桥大学流传着这样的说法，牛顿的猫长得肥，因为他的饭菜总是被猫吃掉。他一个晚上只睡几个小时，而且通常不在床上睡。

牛顿想更多地了解有关行星运行的方式，要做到这一点，他需要一台功能强大的望远镜。然而，在他所处的年代，没有望远镜能满足他的需求。那时的望远镜的工作原理是收集大范围的光线，然后通过玻璃镜片聚焦，这样形成的图像十分模糊，还带有彩色光晕。

牛顿需要的是一个可以更清晰地呈现图像的望远镜，他想运用自己对光的发现解决这个问题。他发现问题出在镜片上。白光穿过镜片时，镜片就犹如一个棱镜，把光分散成了不同颜色的光。这样，光就不能聚焦，形成的图像就很模糊。

牛顿读过另外一种制造望远镜的方式，这要使用镜子。这可能会解决这个问题，因为用镜子，光会受到反射，而不是穿过镜片。然而，当时还没有人真制造过这样的望远镜。

牛顿小时候就喜欢做模型，他用当时所学的技能制造了一个反射望远镜，其效果和比它大十倍的望远镜一样。

第六章

光之争

牛顿发明的神奇望远镜，引起了伦敦一个重要俱乐部的兴趣。这个俱乐部就是英国皇家学会，它建立于 1660 年，由一群学者组成，他们每个星期都会聚在一起观察实验，讨论科学方面的问题。

英国皇家学会认为，知识要往前发展，最佳的途径就是每个人都分享想法，这样一来，每个人的想法就会成为其他人想法的基础，或者和其他人的想法发生碰撞。学会的座右铭是："Nullius in verba."。意思是："别把任何人的话照单全收，自己去思考真理。"

在牛顿所在的时期，涌现了很多类似英国皇家学会的俱乐部，这个时期常被人称为启蒙时代。启蒙意味着，学习改变人们思考方式的重要知识。那个时期伟大的学者们都信奉共同学习，他们想通过理性、逻辑和观察，解决种种问题，而不是靠迷信或宗教。

人们认为，牛顿是启蒙时代的伟大人物，但是他的个性和启蒙理想并不相宜。他不愿倾听他人的建议，只想一个人把工作做到最好。即使在那个时期，他还是很讨厌和别人讨论，如果有人质疑他，甚至认为他的观点是错误的，他就会发脾气。

尽管如此，能有如此重要的团体对他的望远镜感兴趣，还是让牛顿受宠若惊。他在别人的劝说下分享了自己的成果。1671 年，巴罗教授说服他分享望远镜，并在伦敦展示了他的望远镜，这次展示引起了轰动，还惊动了国王。因此，牛顿向英国皇家学会赠送了一台望远镜，作为回报，他获得了学会会员的资格。

1672年，加入了英国皇家学会的牛顿，往前迈出了重要的一步，在行为上他更像启蒙时代的学者了。牛顿不再对自己的研究保密，而是和其他人分享。他给英国皇家学会寄了一篇研究论文，那是他五年前写的有关光学的论文。此外，他还禁不住对自己的重要研究自夸了一番。他骄傲地称其研究为“如果不能称为自然运转中最伟大的发现，那也是最出其不意的研究！”。在论文中，他描述了他所做过的种种实验，并请求英国皇家学会检测他的研究，以验证是否能得出相同的结论。

起初，一切都进展顺利。其中一个成员写信给牛顿，信中说道，他的论文“受到了一致的关注和不同凡响的热烈掌声”。但是，他们也提出了疑问，如，有些人试着做了很多实验，声称实验不成功。这让牛顿感觉他们是在攻击他，因此，他也反击了他们。

英国皇家学会中有一个成员让他尤为生气，这个人名叫罗伯特·胡克。他在学会中的工作职责是，在学会成员相聚的时候，演示实验。胡克其实认同牛顿的大部分观点，但是他认为，牛顿的种种实验并没有真正证明他的观点。

罗伯特·胡克

科学家中有这样的分歧是很常见的，这是一种获得新发现，找到问题解决办法的重要方式。不幸的是，胡克和牛顿都是非常敏感和拥有极强自尊心的人，他们不仅讨论了观点，还因为观点不同而争吵。由于争吵得太厉害，最后演变成了互相侮辱，控告对方剽窃其他人的观点。最终，他们成了彼此的人生宿敌。

牛顿和学者同伴们进行观点分享和讨论交流，但他从未从中获得过愉悦感。他非常想念独自研究获得满足感的日子。“我不想卷入这种恼人而又没有意义的争论。”明确了自己的这种想法后，他重新回到了一个人做研究的工作状态。

第七章

秘密研究

牛顿的问题不仅是和其他学者争吵，他还有个更严重的个人问题。牛顿是剑桥大学的研究员，在那儿生活和工作，剑桥大学给他发薪水，保护他免受外面世界的伤害。然而，剑桥大学是英国教会的一部分，每个剑桥大学的研究员都必须在七年内成为牧师。1674 年，属于牛顿的七年快到期了，因为他心里暗暗不接受教堂的教学，所以他还没有成为牧师。

牛顿信奉基督教，对宗教信仰非常认真。然而，牛顿本人根本不情愿接受他人对重要事情的阐释。

牛顿阅读圣经时，也带着他对自然世界同样强烈的质疑态度。他认为英国教会神圣的三位一体论是讲不通的，因为三位一体论认为，上帝是独一无二的，由圣

父、圣子和圣灵组成，它们是神圣不容置疑的。为了待在剑桥大学，牛顿不得不发誓他认同三位一体论的观点。然而，实际情况是，牛顿根本就不认同。相反，他认为"基督教上帝"的说法是错误的。如果他质疑教会的说法，就会被迫离开剑桥大学，这会让他感到特别耻辱，然而，对待这么重要的事情，他内心又不想欺骗自己。

1675年，牛顿有机会接近国王查理二世。他想，国王是英国教会的领头人，一定能帮他的忙。于是，牛顿没有告诉国王他遇到的问题，而是向国王解释道，他不仅是剑桥大学的成员，还是一名数学教授。基于牛顿的说法，他的意思是说他不需要非成为牧师。尽管他的争辩不是真的有道理，但是查理国王并不在乎，而是做出了决定——牛顿是一名大学教师和数学教授，不需要成为牧师。这样一来，牛顿就可以留在剑桥大学，而且无须撒谎欺骗了。

国王查理二世

正如牛顿有秘密的宗教信仰一样，他也有秘密的科学研究。他想解开炼金术之谜。炼金术一部分是魔法，一部分是宗教，也有一部分是科学。那时，炼金术士们都秘密寻找能把其他金属变成黄金的“哲人之石”和能让人长生不老的“生命灵药”。

牛顿花在炼金术上的时间和精力比花在其他普通科学上的还多。据他的仆人说，牛顿经常彻夜不眠地坐在剑桥的个人实验室里，烧着烈火，神秘地做着各种实验。

这一切似乎都很奇怪，也很令人困惑。一个科学家为什么会参与神秘仪式和魔法实验呢？事实上，要知道炼金术为何令他痴迷，并不难。他讨厌自己的研究受到公众的批判，炼金术则成了他保密的极好借口。炼金术士们认为自己很特别，比普通人更聪明，牛顿喜欢把自己看成精英团队的一员。

然而，牛顿的兴趣不止那些。在牛顿所处的时代，科学的发展仍然处于初级阶段。人们不能区分神话和事实，炼金术士们相信，他们能把其他任何金属炼成黄金。他们认为，万物都是由微小的颗粒组成的，这些颗粒可以被分解并组合成其他东西。

炼金术士们提出的问题并不愚蠢，他们的一些炼金术知识最终发展成了现代化学，并有助于我们了解原子是如何形成分子的。

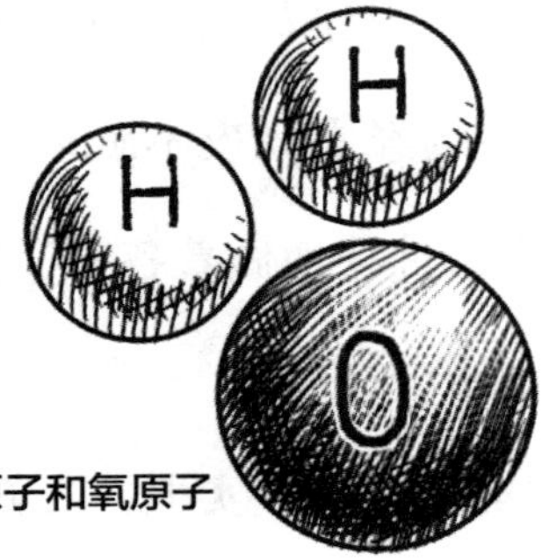

氢原子和氧原子

水分子

那个时代仍然是启蒙时代，严肃的思想家正在摒弃只有少数被选中的人才能获得特殊秘密智慧的观念。牛顿去世后，英国皇家学会发现他写了超过一百万字的有关炼金术的文章，他们因此感到特别尴尬，于是在这些文章上标注“不宜出版的文章”。直到 2004 年，牛顿有关炼金术的文章才得以出版。

第八章

一场证明竞争

和英国皇家学会的争论结束后，牛顿退出了。他专注于秘密研究炼金术，并声称自己不会再对科学研究感兴趣了。也许他当时说这话是认真的，但是，他最伟大的科学成就还在后面。

1684 年，三个英国皇家学会成员在一家咖啡馆讨论当时的科学问题。这三个人中，一个是他的敌人胡克，一个是叫埃德蒙 · 哈雷的年轻炼金术士，还有一个是著名的建筑师克里斯托弗 · 雷恩。雷恩一直试图弄明白行星是如何以及为什么围绕太阳运转的，他

埃德蒙 · 哈雷

克里斯托弗·雷恩

现在正在向其他两个人求助。

那时，人们已经知道行星运行的实际轨迹。早在 1609 年，约翰尼斯·开普勒就已经证明了行星的运行轨迹是椭圆的。人们还知道行星和太阳之间的作用力的大小决定了行星运行轨迹的路径。但是其中还牵扯到一些其他问题，没有人能弄清楚。作用力的变化十分复杂，有赖于两个天体之间的距离远近。随着行星和太阳之间的距离越来越大，作用力也就变得越来越小。这有一定道理，但是作用力和距离似乎并没有以相同的速度发生变化。距离越远，作用力变化得越快，没有人确切地知道距离和作用力之间真正的关系。

学者们提出了不同的观点来解释它们之间的关系。其中一种观点是，距离和作用力之间是一种数学关系，叫作平方反比律关系。雷恩认为，这种描述可能是正确的，但当他试图去证明这一点时，却无法做到。

雷恩将这个问题讲给他的朋友们听，期待着他们能够用数学方法证明平方反比律能算出椭圆轨迹。如果能证明这一关系，就意味着，他们发现了有关行星运行的重要新规律。

胡克吹牛说，他已经这样计算过了，但是不想和其他人分享他的计算。首先，他希望其他人去做实验，去体验失败；然后，他再展示给他们看如何做实验。雷恩和哈雷并不欣赏胡克（因为当牛顿展示奇妙无比的望远镜时，胡克声称，他本人已经有了一台功能更好的望远镜，体积特别小，能挂在他的表链上）。因此，雷恩提出了奖赏——最先用数学方法证明作用力和距离关系的人将获得一本价值连城的书。

两个月后，胡克还是没有给雷恩展示如何证明作用力和距离的关系。于是，怀着紧张的心情，哈雷决定去找容易发脾气的牛顿。结果，牛顿和胡克一样，声称他多年前就已经证明了平方反比律能够证明椭圆轨迹的运行。不幸的是，他忘记把证明手稿放哪儿了。当时，他只是为了好玩才去证明的，不过，他承诺，一旦发现手稿，就会寄给哈雷。和胡克不一样的是，牛顿并没有吹牛说假话。几个月后，牛顿果真给哈雷寄去了证明手稿。

哈雷彗星

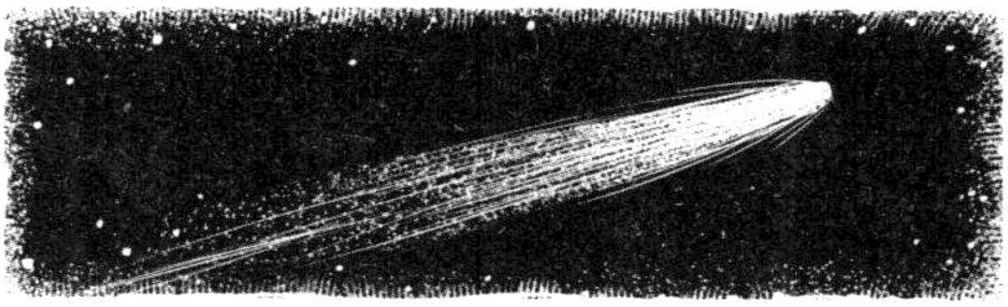

彗星是天空中像恒星一样明亮的天体，通常有一条长长的尾巴。在牛顿所处的时代，人们认为，只要看到彗星，就意味着要发生糟糕的事情或美妙的事情。1682 年，人们看到了彗星。结果，牛顿的朋友埃德蒙·哈雷看到了多年以前天文学家的报道。他注意到大概每隔七十六年，就会出现有关天空中出现明亮物体的报道。埃德蒙·哈雷大胆推测，报道中提及的天空中多次出现的彗星，一定是同一颗彗星。这就意味着，彗星和行星一样，是绕着太阳运行的，只是彗星的轨道要长得多。因此，他预测，彗星将于 1758 年再次出现，到那时，哈雷早已不在人世。然而，正如哈雷预测的那样，彗星在 1758 年再次出现，人们便以他的名字命名了这颗彗星。

第九章

牛顿巨著出版

哈雷提出的问题重新点燃了牛顿对行星运行方式的兴趣，他为此写了一篇九页的论文来回答这个问题，并继续研究下去。“既然我在研究这个问题，”他在论文中写道，“我会欣然研究到底。”牛顿只花了十八个月的时间就完成五百页篇幅的巨著，这本书的名字叫《自然哲学的数学原理》，拉丁文书名为《原理》，通过这本书，他奠定了现代物理学的基础。自 1687 年以后，所有物理学家都是以牛顿这本著作中的观点为基础进行研究的。

哈雷为牛顿写的这篇巨著感到兴奋不已。为了确保牛顿不会

把研究成果只局限于自己知晓，他做了牛顿的编辑，甚至还出资出版了牛顿的巨著。

麻烦似乎如影随形。牛顿的书一经出版，宿敌胡克就宣称牛顿剽窃了他的观点。牛顿因此感到怒不可遏，发誓不再出版任何作品。最终，哈雷想尽一切办法才让牛顿心情平静下来。

牛顿的书出版于 1687 年，一经出版就引起了轰动。读者觉得，突然之间，宇宙就被解释得很清楚。一个法国数学家读过他的书后，提出疑问："牛顿先生和其他人一样吃饭、喝水、睡觉吗？"（正如人们所知，这个问题的回答是不。）

崇拜这本书和讨论这本书的人可能比真正读过这本书的人要多，因为读者几乎是读不懂这本书的。牛顿甚至暗示过，他是故意这样写的。因为他认为这是一种保护他自己的方式，是保护他免受他人愚蠢质疑的一种方式。

牛顿的书出版后，他一举成名，被选为了议会会员。他成了政府成员后，正好赶上投票支持 1689 年的光荣革命。尽管他表现得并不积极，在议会中唯一说过的话就是让人关窗户。然而，正是因为有了他重要的一票，英国才产生了新一任国王。

第十章

三大运动定律

牛顿的巨著出版以来，已经过去了三百多年，难以想象他出版的巨著的影响力有多大。他当时弄清楚了的问题，对现在的我们来说，是自然的，也是显而易见的。因为牛顿的观点完全改变了人的思考方式。如今，即使是从未听说过牛顿的人，也会用他创造的术语描述运动。

牛顿出版的革命性巨著到底写了什么呢？首先写了万有引力定律。早先，牛顿研究过两种力量，第一种是吸引苹果掉落和吸引月球与地球保持一定距离的力量；第二种是使行星围绕太阳转动的力量。牛顿认为，这两种力量其实就是一种力量。他给这种力量命了名，当今的人们依然在使用这个名称。“现在，明确了这种力量叫作万有引力。因此，从今往后，我们可以称之为万有引力了。”

在这本巨著中，牛顿还写了三大运动定律。第一大运动定律是他从伽利略那里学习到的。如果物体在运动，它会保持运动，除非有外力迫使它停止运动；反之，如果物体是静止的，那么它会保持静止，除非有外力迫使它运动起来。

巨著中的第二大运动定律说明了使物体运动或静止需要多大的力。

第三大运动定律则认为：“每一个作用力都有一个大小相等、方向相反的反作用力。”这意味着当你用力推挤什么东西时，它都会以同样的力度反向推挤你。

比如说，如果你站在滑板上，用脚推地面，地面会以相反的方向推你，这就是滑板能向前滑动的原因。还有，如果你给一个充满了空气的气球放气，空气就会向后从气球里喷出去。

空气会以相同大小的力推动气球前进，因此气球就在空中飞起来了。这种原理使火箭引擎能正常工作。

作用力
反作用力

牛顿的三大运动定律解释了宇宙中所有事物的运行。这些定律和很多数学知识结合时，就能够预测地球上的潮汐运动和遥远星际中行星的运行。

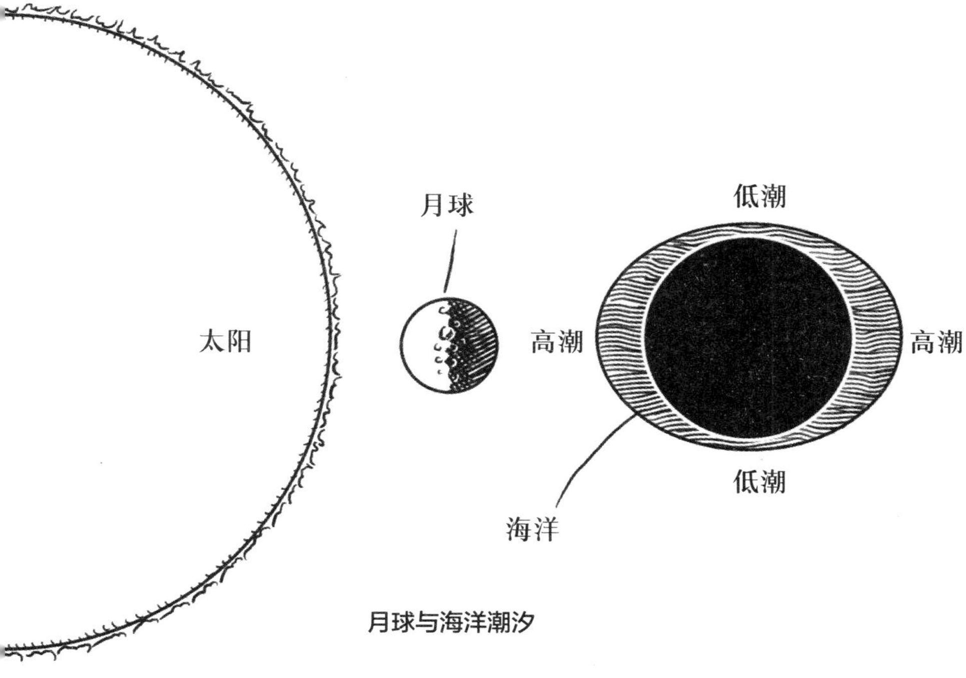

月球与海洋潮汐

让人感到奇怪的是，牛顿的巨著对万有引力的解释存在不足。尽管牛顿描述了万有引力是如何起作用的，但是他从未清楚地说明万有引力到底是什么。我们不能因此责怪牛顿，因为三百年过去了，我们也没有真正弄明白万有引力是什么。

第十一章

成就传奇

牛顿的书出版后，他就变成了传奇人物。剑桥大学的学生突然间都以一种全新的眼光看他。“我们注视他……犹如注视圣人一样。”一个学生这样回忆道。

然而，牛顿的生活在接下来的几年里，一如往常。到了 1693 年，他经历了一次精神疾病，这导致他无法正常就餐和就寝。牛顿还写信给他的朋友，令人感到奇怪的是，他在信中写他希望他们早点去死，还指责朋友试图让他陷入与女人的麻烦关系中。

精神得到恢复后，牛顿决定改变自己。1696 年，他委托了一些有权势的朋友帮他找一份新工作。最后，他们安排他去管理皇家铸币厂。

伦敦塔

皇家铸币厂是制造英国所有硬币的地方。铸币厂就在伦敦塔里面，牛顿因此搬到了伦敦的一个大房子里住。他的朋友认为他会雇另一个人做大部分工作，然而事实刚好相反，牛顿本人全身心地投入到了这项工作中。

多年来，硬币伪造者会剪下真硬币边缘的银来制造假硬币。到了牛顿所在的时期，英国的大部分货币的价值都不如预期了。因此，政府不得不采取措施。1696年，政府决定铸造新硬币。

皇家铸币厂回收了所有被剪了边缘的硬币，把它们制造成新硬币。这些硬币边缘呈山脊状，所以很难伪造，牛顿监管了铸造新硬币的完整过程。他在皇家铸币厂表现卓越，1699年被提拔为铸币厂厂长。他在这个职位上待了近三十年，直到他去世。

铸造新硬币的伟大工作一结束，牛顿就专注于抓捕硬币伪造者。他变成了一个拥有间谍和线人网络的侦探。牛顿在侦探工作上最伟大的成就是抓捕了狡猾的硬币伪造者：查洛纳。牛顿追捕他多年，最终将他绳之以法。

牛顿在伦敦最初的几年里，一直和英国皇家学会保持距离，因为他不想再有争论。1703 年，他的宿敌胡克去世。此外，英国皇家学会会长也于同年去世。他们去世后，牛顿立即被推选为会长。1704 年，牛顿终于出版了他的光学理论之书。这本书是基于他多年前的研究成果写成的。然而，正如他自己解释的那样："为了避免在这些问题上发生争执，我推迟了本书的出版。"实际上，牛顿做出解释的意思是，他一直等到胡克去世才出版了这本书。

第十二章

英国皇家学会的争论

牛顿像暴君一样管理着英国皇家学会，这导致了一些丑闻。最糟糕的丑闻莫过于争论是谁真正发明了微积分。牛顿早在 1665 年就创造了微积分，即流数法，但是他当时拒绝出版这些内容。只有精心挑选过的人才有机会看到他写的内容。

戈特弗里德·莱布尼茨

大概在 1675 年，一个名叫戈特弗里德·莱布尼茨的德国数学家提出了相似的方法，他称之为微积分。有人和牛顿有相同的发现，这并不令人惊讶。毕竟，莱布尼茨一直致力于解决相同的问题。莱布尼茨甚至还写信给牛顿，介绍自己在数学方面的新发现（具有讽刺意味的是，他在一封信中是这样开头的：我想我太感激您了……）。1684 年，莱布尼茨发表了他有关微积分的论文。

刚开始，一切似乎都很好。牛顿在 1704 年终于出版了他的微积分著作。一位匿名审稿人暗示，牛顿可能抄袭了莱布尼茨的观点。

牛顿得知后，怒火难遏。因此，他不允许任何人获得发现微积分的荣誉。就这样，牛顿控告莱布尼茨剽窃了他的观点，两个人之间进行了一场丑陋的斗争。一开始，莱布尼茨非常讲道理。“牛顿进一步发展了微积分，但是我用另一种方式发现了微积分，”他在写给一个朋友的信中写道，“这个人做了这样的贡献，那个人做了那样的贡献。”

牛顿认为这没有任何区别。“二次发现者，”牛顿声称，“没有权利。”

最后，在 1711 年，莱布尼茨请求英国皇家学会解决两人的斗争。但是，牛顿是英国皇家学会会长，他亲自负责这个调查问题的委员会。此外，他还秘密地撰写了委员会报告。

1713年，牛顿公开发表了委员会报告，报告歪曲了事实，似乎向大众表明：是莱布尼茨剽窃了他的观点。莱布尼茨在三年后去世了。牛顿似乎从未后悔他的所作所为。多年后，牛顿还兴高采烈地回忆道："我曾经让莱布尼茨伤心欲绝。"

然而，从某种意义上来说，莱布尼茨获得了微积分斗争的胜利。牛顿的流数法只是一种个人的简化符号，他从未考虑过他人要如何借鉴使用，而人们更容易理解莱布尼茨的观点体系。因此，当今任何微积分学习者都在使用莱布尼茨的术语、符号和方法，并没有使用牛顿的简化符号。甚至微积分这个词都是莱布尼茨提出的，如果牛顿知道这一点，他一定会再次怒火难遏。

第十三章

天才

尽管牛顿幼时体弱多病，却活到了老年。在他的晚年，他富有、有权势、受人尊敬。1705 年，安妮女王授予了他爵士称号，他成为艾萨克·牛顿爵士。

牛顿一向是个思想尖锐、身体健康的人。去世前不到一个月的时候，他还召开了一次英国皇家学会会议。

牛顿于 1727 年 3 月 20 日去世，享年八十五岁。他被安葬在伦敦威斯敏斯特教堂，他是英国第一个获此殊荣的科学家。大理石墓碑上雕刻着后人对他表达敬重的碑文："此地为艾萨克·牛顿爵士之墓，他的思想近乎神圣……不断探索……探索其他学者未曾想过的东西。"伟大诗人亚历山大·蒲柏为牛顿所写的碑文是："自然与自然之法深藏于黑夜。上帝说：'让牛顿去黑夜里探索吧！'此后，黑夜都将变白昼。"

牛顿的思想近乎神圣——这样的评价很高，牛顿所在的时代以及我们这个时代的科学家都这样评价他。牛顿取得的成就比他获得的个人发现更伟大，他想弄清楚万事万物是如何结合在一起的。这就好似其他学者写下了一些有趣的观点，而牛顿就是那个找到了一种方式能整合所有人的观点并告知人们宇宙是怎样运转的人。

威斯敏斯特教堂

威斯敏斯特教堂重修于1245年，是当时的国王、女王及皇室成员结婚和加冕的地方。直到18世纪60年代，这里也是他们去世后安葬的地方。安葬在这里的还有威斯敏斯特教堂的工作服务人员。牛顿在童年时期就知道，安葬在威斯敏斯特教堂是一种纪念有特别大成就的人的方式。伟大的将军、政治家、诗人和音乐家都是以这种方式得到认可的，艾萨克·牛顿是第一个获得这种纪念方式的科学家。

牛顿知道，他只是开始讲述这个故事。作为一个老人，他说："我不知道在世人看来我是什么样的人，但就我自己而言，我似乎只是一个在海边玩耍的男孩，时不时地发现一块比普通石头更光滑的鹅卵石或一个更漂亮的贝壳，以此来转移自己的注意力，而真理的汪洋大海就在我面前，一切都还没有被发现。"

在接下来的两百年里，几乎所有的物理学发展都源于他的思想。直到 20 世纪初，另一个伟大的天才阿尔伯特·爱因斯坦发现了牛顿物理学的局限性。然而，在日常生活中，人们很少会遇到牛顿物理学不合理的情况。它仍然是我们理解世界的方式。无论我们是在骑自行车、接棒球，还是摔苹果，我们大多数人都会用从那个奇怪的、脾气不好

阿尔伯特·爱因斯坦

的、才华横溢的独行人艾萨克·牛顿那里学到的术语来思考运动。

艾萨克·牛顿生平年表

1642 年	艾萨克 · 牛顿于 12 月 25 日出生。
1654 年	搬到附近的镇就读文法学校。
1661 年	进入剑桥大学三一学院。
1665 年	获剑桥大学学士学位。
	回母亲的农场避瘟疫。
1668 年	获剑桥大学硕士学位。
1669 年	获卢卡斯学院的数学教授席位。
1671 年	给英国皇家学会赠送反射望远镜。
1672 年	当选英国皇家学会会员。
1679 年	母亲汉娜去世。
1684 年	哈雷、胡克和雷恩在咖啡馆讨论行星运行。
1687 年	出版《自然哲学的数学原理》著作。
1689 年	获议会会员资格。
1693 年	患精神疾病。
1696 年	到伦敦铸币厂工作。
1699 年	任铸币厂厂长。
1703 年	任英国皇家学会会长。
1704 年	出版光学著作。
1705 年	被封为爵士。
1712 年	英国皇家学会设立委员会确定微积分发明者。
1727 年	艾萨克 · 牛顿于 3 月 20 日去世。

世界大事记

1642 年 — 英国内战爆发。
1648 年 — 持续三十年的欧洲战争结束。
1649 年 — 1 月 30 日，查理国王被斩首。
1660 年 — 英国查理二世复辟。
— 英国皇家学会成立。
1663 年 — 罗伯特 · 胡克发明“细胞”一词描述他用望远镜看到的东西。
1665 年 — 英国大瘟疫暴发。
1666 年 — 伦敦发生大火。
1667 年 — 弥尔顿出版《失乐园》。
1670 年 — 英国人在北美建立查尔斯顿（最初名为查尔斯城镇）。
1675 年 — 怀表被发明出来。
1682 年 — 哈雷彗星出现。
1688—1689 年 — 英国光荣革命。
1689 年 — 一项权利法案保障了英国人言论和宗教方面的某些自由。
1692 年 — 塞勒姆女巫案的审判在马萨诸塞州进行。
1694 年 — 英格兰银行建立。
1706 年 — 本杰明 · 富兰克林出生。
1709 年 — “大霜冻”是欧洲五百多年来最寒冷的冬天。
1712 年 — 第一台实用蒸汽机被制造出来。
1727 年 — 珍妮特 · 霍恩成为英国最后一个被处决的“女巫”。

Who Was Isaac Newton?

In 1665, a terrible sickness swept through England. It was called the plague. It caused huge swellings all over the body and made people's skin turn black. There was no cure. Most people who caught it died a quick and painful death. Any place people lived crowded together was dangerous, because plague was very easy to catch. No one knew what caused it, or how to protect themselves against it. The only way to stay safe was to go to the countryside, where there were fewer people to catch it from.

A twenty-three-year-old student named Isaac Newton had to leave Cambridge University and flee to his mother's farmhouse. He didn't really mind. He had always been a loner. He didn't have friends he would miss. At his mother's house, he spent the time doing what he did best—thinking about the universe.

One day he saw an apple fall. He began to wonder what pulled the apple toward the Earth. And so, according to the famous legend (which might even be true), young Isaac Newton thought up the idea of gravity.

The plague years were a terrible time for most people, but not for Newton. For him, they were a wonderful time of discovery, and not just about gravity. He came up with enough new ideas to keep him busy thinking and writing for the rest of his life. His ideas helped people understand how the universe worked in a new way.

After eighteen months, Newton went back to Cambridge, but he never did make many friends. He was jealous and unfriendly, and he lost his temper easily. He wasn't a very nice person, but he was one of the greatest scientific geniuses who has ever lived.

Chapter 1

Lonely Boy

Isaac Newton was born in Lincolnshire, England, on Christmas Day 1642. (Because England used a different calendar then, his birthday is also given as January 4, 1643.) He didn't seem to have a great future. At first, it didn't seem he had any future at all. He was born too early. He was weak and so tiny he could fit into a quart mug. No one thought the sickly baby would live, but he did. His father, also named Isaac, had died three months before his son's birth. He had been a well-off farmer, but he couldn't read or write—not even enough to sign his name.

When Isaac was only three, his mother, Hannah, got married again, to a minister named Barnabas Smith. Smith

The English Civil War

Newton was born right at the beginning of the English Civil War. During his childhood, the king and parliament were locked in a bloody struggle. In 1649, when Newton was six, King Charles I was put on trial and beheaded. A strict government with no king took power. Eleven years later, in 1660, the monarchy was restored under Charles II. Although Newton's family was not personally involved in the war, the violence and uncertainty of the time had an impact on his childhood.

wanted a wife, but not a son. Hannah agreed to move into her new husband's house, leaving Isaac behind with her parents.

Little Isaac almost never saw his mother, and he was very lonely. Sometimes he would climb a tree so he could stare at his mother's new home. He hated his stepfather so much that he imagined burning down the house with him in it. When Isaac was ten, however, his stepfather died. His mother moved back, bringing with her a half brother and two half sisters for Isaac.

Isaac went to the little local village school, which didn't teach much beyond how to read. He seemed unusually intelligent, so Hannah decided to send him to a better school. The King's School was seven miles away—too far to walk—so Isaac lived with the Clarke family in town. The family later said that while he lived there, Isaac fell in love with Clarke's daughter Catherine. If this is true, she was the only girlfriend he ever had. Years later Catherine remembered him as "a sober, silent, thinking lad" who was never known to "play with the boys . . . at their silly amusements." In his spare time, he built doll furniture for Catherine.

Clarke was an apothecary. An apothecary is someone who makes medicine by combining herbs and chemicals. This involved careful work with weights and measures, as well as knowing what was special about different substances. Young Isaac was fascinated. By watching and perhaps helping Clarke, he began to learn basic chemistry—how different things interact with each other. He even created his own potions, such as a medicine made up of turpentine, rosewater, beeswax, olive oil, a kind of wine called sack, and red sandalwood. This was meant to protect him from a deadly disease called tuberculosis.

Isaac was also fascinated by ways to keep track of time. The clocks of the day weren't very accurate, and he thought he could do a better job. He charted the movement of shadows from sunrise to sunset. Then he hammered pegs into the wall to create a sundial. When people wanted to know the real time, they'd check "Isaac's dial." For telling time indoors, he designed a clock with a wooden dial turned by the steady dripping of water. He also built a tiny windmill, with a mouse to run it.

Unfortunately, the subjects taught at school didn' t interest him. He didn't study, and he was at the bottom of his class. One day a boy who was a good student kicked him in the stomach. Isaac immediately challenged him to a fight, which, to everyone's surprise, he won. Isaac was very good at holding a grudge. Just winning the fight wasn't enough for him. He wanted to beat his enemy in school as well, so he finally began to study. Soon he rose to the top of the class.

The main subjects at school were Latin and Greek. Both would be useful to him later on, because almost all the most important books and articles were still written in these languages. He may have also learned some simple, useful arithmetic and geometry.

Hannah thought of education mainly as a way to make

her son a good farmer. Soon she decided it was time for him to practice running a farm, so she took him out of school. The idea of growing crops and taking care of animals bored Isaac. He deliberately did a bad job.

When he was supposed to be working, he sat under a hedge reading or building things. Once when he was supposed to watch the sheep, he let them run into a neighbor's field and eat the crops.

His mother was hauled into court and had to pay a fine after that happened. Isaac was not turning into the kind of farmer his mother hoped for.

Chapter 2

Cambridge

Luckily, Isaac wasn't the only one who hated the idea of his becoming a farmer. The master of his school thought it was a waste of a brilliant mind. Along with Isaac's uncle, he managed to talk Hannah into letting her son go to a university. So at eighteen, Isaac Newton left for Trinity College. This was part of Cambridge University. He would spend the next forty years living there, first as a student and then as a professor.

Newton's first months at Cambridge were a letdown. Even though Hannah was well-off, she didn't want to pay his fees, so he had to enter as what was called a sizar. This meant he worked as a servant to the richer students.

Most of them were more interested in having a good time than in learning. Newton despised them. He grew less lonely when he met another serious student, John Wickins. They moved in with each other and lived together for the next twenty years. Wickins was one of the few people Newton ever stayed friends with for long. Unfortunately Wickins never wrote down his memories of Newton.

Study at Cambridge was still based on ancient Greek and Latin philosophy, especially the writings of the Greek philosopher Aristotle. Aristotle was a brilliant man— the Newton of his time—but he had lived in the fourth century BC. Over two thousand years later, knowledge in many areas hadn't moved much beyond what he taught.

Aristotle based his theories on observation of the world around him. However, it was even more important to him for an idea to make sense. He didn't always test his ideas against reality. For instance, he thought that human males, being bigger and stronger, would have more teeth than human

Cambridge

In Newton's time, very few people actually got to go to college. There were only two universities in all of England: Oxford and Cambridge. Both were ancient. Their main purpose was to prepare students to be ministers in the Church of England, and only members of the Church were allowed to attend them. Every student had a personal tutor who took charge of his education. Many of the upper-class students, however, were only there to have a good time.

females. That seemed reasonable to him. If he had actually looked in men's and women's mouths, he would have seen that he was wrong. In the centuries after his death, other scholars often just accepted what Aristotle had said as the truth.

Much of what was taught at Cambridge didn't interest Newton, and he paid little attention to it. What Cambridge did offer was a library full of books.

Over the past few centuries, daring scholars had been challenging the old ways of explaining how the world worked. The word *scientist* hadn't been invented yet—these scholars were known as natural philosophers. They became the founders of modern science. Newton set out to learn from them.

Newton read the ideas of Nicolaus Copernicus, one scholar who challenged Aristotle. Aristotle thought that the Earth was the center of the universe and all the other heavenly bodies moved around it. In the sixteenth century, Copernicus suggested it made more sense to think that the Earth and all the other planets moved around the sun. This seemed reasonable to Newton.

Aristotle's idea felt right—it certainly looks to us like everything revolves around the Earth. But anyone who actually watched the planets in the sky could see that sometimes the way they moved didn't match what Aristotle described.

People came up with all sorts of complicated ideas to explain why the planets didn't behave as Aristotle said they should. But if they stopped trying to force the planets into Aristotle's system and switched to Copernicus's system, with all the planets traveling around the sun, everything suddenly made sense. The planets moved just the way Copernicus's theory predicted.

Newton also read the work of Johannes Kepler, who had built on Copernicus's work.

Copernicus had suggested that planets moved in circles around the sun. Kepler tracked the planets' movements carefully and discovered their exact paths. They were not circles but a kind of oval called an ellipse.

Then there was Galileo, an Italian who died the year Newton was born. He looked at the heavens through a telescope and reported on the surprising things he saw. For instance, the moon was covered with mountains and craters, and there were spots on the sun. Aristotle said that heavenly bodies must be pure and more perfect than anything on Earth. What Galileo actually saw made him disagree. Even out beyond the moon, it looked as if things were made of the same ordinary material as on Earth.

Galileo believed in testing the truth of what other people told him. For instance, Aristotle said that heavy objects fell faster than light objects. That certainly sounds reasonable, but Galileo wondered if they really did. He came up with experiments to find out, by dropping balls and measuring how fast they fell. According to legend, Galileo dropped balls from the leaning Tower of Pisa. That isn't so. Nevertheless, he did discover that Aristotle was wrong. Objects of the same size and shape, dropped from the same height, fall at the same speed, no matter how much—or how little—they weigh.

From reading these men's works, Newton learned something. It didn't matter how reasonable an idea seemed. It had to match what could actually be observed. If the world didn't do what an idea said it would, it was time to come up with a new idea.

At Cambridge, Newton began to teach himself mathematics. This interest grew out of a visit to Stourbridge Fair. The fair was a huge outdoor gathering with farmers and tradesmen selling everything from farm animals to clothing to toys. Full of young couples, dancers, and performing animals, it was a much more frivolous place than Newton usually liked. But he did find a bookseller there, and he bought a book on astrology.

Astrology is the belief that the stars and planets rule people's lives. Astrologers use the heavens to predict the future and try to control events on Earth. Astrology had become very complicated, using elaborate calculations and charts.

Many people in Newton's time believed in astrology, so he was curious about it. Before he had read very far in his new book, Newton came to an example that used a kind of difficult mathematics he didn't know. He bought another book to teach himself about it. But before he could understand this new book, he had to know a more basic branch of mathematics that he hadn't learned yet. So he had to back up and start at the beginning.

In 1665, Newton passed the exams for his bachelor's degree. His grades were not very good. Most of the exam questions were about subjects that didn't interest him. Still he did well enough to become a scholar. This meant he could keep living and studying at Cambridge, with free room and board. Almost as soon as he earned the right to stay at Cambridge, however, he had to leave.

Chapter 3

The Plague Years

In 1665, the plague broke out in England. The university was closed, and Newton went home to Lincolnshire.

For the next eighteen months, he lived at home. Newton had never much liked being with other people. He was happy to be left alone to think about exactly what he wanted. This was the most productive time of Newton's life. He later remembered, "In those days I was in my prime of age for invention." By *invention* he meant being able to think up new ideas.

What was he thinking up? A new kind of mathematics, to start with. The math he knew was fine to use for some kinds of problems. If you knew how fast a wagon was going and that it was moving in a circle, it was easy to figure out where it would be an hour later. However, Newton was interested in a different kind of problem. He wondered about things that were changing all the time. What if you shot a cannonball into the air? First it would travel in a curve upward, slowing down more and more. Then it would get to the top of its path and start curving back down toward the Earth. As it got nearer to the ground, it would move faster and faster. Its speed and its direction were always changing. How could you create a mathematical equation that would describe this kind of movement when it was never the same for an instant?

Newton invented his own form of mathematics—one that could handle this kind of question. He called it the *method of fluxions*. Fluxion means "continual change." Today we call his invention calculus. Modern physics, the study of motion, matter, and energy, would not be possible without it.

Another subject that always interested Newton was

The Plague and the Great Fire

When the plague struck, London became a city of death. As many as one in five people were killed by the disease. Then in September 1666, just as the plague was beginning to die down, a great fire broke out. Starting in a bakery, it burned for three days. Most people managed to escape, but 80 percent of the buildings in London were ruined. Although no one knew it, the plague was carried by rats and fleas. By destroying all the filthy old buildings where the rats lived, the fire may have helped end the plague.

light. He had bought himself a prism at Stourbridge Fair. This was a specially shaped piece of glass. When light shone through it, the light turned into a rainbow of color. (We call this the spectrum.) Newton began playing around with his prism, testing what he had learned about light.

Aristotle taught that in its basic form, light was pure white. All other colors came from making changes to white light. If you changed it a little, you got red. Changing it a little more gave you orange, and so on through all the colors. But by now, Newton knew Aristotle was sometimes wrong. Maybe he was wrong about light.

Newton knew that when you shine white light through a prism, the light breaks up into all the colors of the spectrum. What would happen if you sent the broken-up spectrum through a second prism? If white light was really being changed to turn into all the colors, a second prism should change the light even more. Newton discovered that, in fact, this didn't happen. A second prism brought all the colors back together to create a single beam of white light again.

This made Newton think of other questions. What would happen if you shone just a single color of light through a second prism? He created an experiment to find out. First he passed a ray of white light through a prism, to get the whole spectrum. Then he took just the green light and sent it through a second prism. If Aristotle was right, the first prism had already done something to the white light that had turned it green. What would the second prism do? Would it break the green light up into the whole spectrum again? Would it just change the green a little more, so it turned blue? Instead, Newton discovered that the second prism made no change at all. The green beam stayed green.

His experiments told Newton that Aristotle was wrong. White light was not the basic form of light. Instead, white light was made up of all the different colors put together. The prism wasn't making changes to the white light. It was breaking it up and separating it into its different parts.

From what he figured out about light, Newton was able to explain a mystery. Until Newton, no one understood what made rainbows appear in the sky. Newton realized that drops of water in the air could act like prisms, breaking the white light of the sun into red, orange, yellow, green, blue, indigo, and violet. He was able to explain how, when sunlight passed through these natural prisms, it created a rainbow.

Chapter 4

Falling Apples

Newton's year at his mother's house came to be called his *annus mirabilis*. In Latin that means *miraculous year*. It seemed like a miracle that one young man could figure out so much in so short a time. Discovering the true nature of light and inventing calculus was just the beginning. He also began the work that would lead to the laws of motion named after him and to the theory of gravity. The famous story about Newton tells how a falling apple led him to discover gravity. This story may even be true. In his later years, Newton himself said his first notion of gravity was "occasioned by the fall of an apple," and there were apple trees at Woolsthorpe.

Aristotle taught that the reason things fall is because

heavy objects have a natural tendency to move downward. Again it seemed to Newton that Aristotle was wrong. He didn't think it made sense to say that objects had a built-in need to fall down. He thought there must be some kind of force that pulled things toward the Earth.

If there was such a force, how far up could it reach? Newton decided that maybe the force didn't have any limits. The very same force that pulled on the apple could also be pulling on the moon and the planets as well.

This was a brand-new and amazing idea. In Newton's time, people thought the universe was divided into two parts. There were forces that worked here on Earth and there were forces out beyond the moon. They were completely different. Because people couldn't travel to outer space, there was no way to study these forces. This meant no one could ever learn how the universe worked beyond the small part people could reach.

Now Newton had decided that if he studied the falling

apple, he could learn about the forces at work on everything in the universe. The more he thought about it, the more certain he became. The force that made an apple fall from a tree was the very same force that made the moon circle around the Earth instead of flying off into space.

No one knows exactly how far Newton got in figuring out all these ideas during his miraculous year, or how much he worked out later. It was a long time before Newton shared his thoughts with anyone else.

All his life Newton hated going public with his discoveries. He didn't like to tell anyone else until he was positive he had worked out every detail perfectly. He wanted to be sure no one could possibly catch him making a mistake. He also seemed to like keeping his bold, exciting ideas all to himself.

Chapter 5

The Wonderful Telescope

When the plague finally ended in 1667, Newton went back to Cambridge. Here one of his teachers encouraged him to share at least one of his discoveries with the world. This teacher was Isaac Barrow, the first-ever professor of mathematics at Cambridge.

In 1669, Newton showed Barrow a paper he had written on his method of fluxions. Barrow was amazed by this wonderful new mathematical tool. He thought it was too important for Newton to keep all to himself. Newton reluctantly let Barrow show the paper to a very small number of people, but he absolutely refused to let it be published.

In October 1669, Barrow left Cambridge. He thought

so highly of Newton that he arranged for Newton to take his place as professor of mathematics. Thanks to Barrow, Newton was finally able to live exactly the kind of life he wanted. His duties didn't take much time or energy. All he had to do was give a few lectures. He was a very dull lecturer and difficult to understand. Almost no one went to hear him.

Newton didn't care. He wasn't interested in the other students or professors. He spent most of his time wandering around the university in badly fitting clothing, with his long silver hair hanging uncombed.

Newton was often so busy thinking that he would forget whether or not he had eaten. The rumor at Cambridge was that his cat got fat from the meals Newton left sitting on his table. He slept only a few hours a night and often not in his bed.

Newton wanted to learn more about the way planets moved. To do this, he needed a powerful telescope, but the telescopes of his time weren't good enough for him. They worked by collecting light from a wide area and then focusing it through a glass lens. The images they produced were fuzzy, with a fringe of colors.

Newton wanted a telescope that gave a clearer image. He used what he had discovered about light to solve the problem. The trouble was the lens, he realized. When white light passed through a lens, the lens acted like a prism and broke the light into separate colors. This caused the light to become unfocused, and the image would blur.

Newton had read about another possible way to make a telescope, one that used a mirror. This might get around the problem, because the light would be reflected, instead of passing through a lens. But no one had ever managed to actually build such a telescope.

Newton had loved to build models when he was a child. He used the skills he had learned then to make a reflecting telescope that worked as well as telescopes ten times its size.

Chapter 6

Fighting about Light

Newton's wonderful telescope caught the interest of an important club in London. It was called the Royal Society. Founded in 1660, this was a group of scholars who met every week to watch experiments and talk about science.

The Royal Society thought the best way to advance knowledge was to discuss ideas, so each man could build on— or knock down—what the others were thinking. Their motto was *Nullius in verba*, which means roughly, "Don't take anyone's word for it."

Clubs like the Royal Society were springing up all over in Newton's time. This period is often called the Age of Enlightenment. *Enlightenment* means learning the kind of important knowledge that changes the way people think. The great scholars of the time believed in working together. They wanted to deal with issues of all kinds using reason, logic, and observation—not superstition or religion.

Newton is considered one of the Enlightenment's greatest figures, but his personality didn't fit the Enlightenment ideal very well. He didn't want advice from other people. He wanted to keep his work to himself until it was perfect. Even then, he hated talking about it with other people. If they questioned him—or even worse, thought he might be wrong—he lost his temper.

Still it was flattering for Newton to have such an important group interested in his telescope. He let himself be persuaded to share. In 1671, Barrow displayed the telescope in London, where it was a huge hit—even with the king. Newton donated a telescope to the Royal Society. In return, the society made him a member.

Joining the Royal Society in 1672 led Newton to take

another important step. He would try to behave more like an Enlightenment scholar. Instead of keeping his research secret, he would share it with others. He sent the fellows of the Royal Society a paper about the research on light he had done five years earlier. He couldn't resist bragging a little about how important the work was. He proudly described it as "the oddest if not the most considerable detection which hath hitherto been made in the operations of nature." He described the experiments he had done and asked the society members to see if they could get the same results.

At first, all seemed well. One member wrote to Newton that his paper had " met with a singular attention and uncommon applause." However, not everyone agreed with everything he said. They had questions. Some people tried his experiments and claimed they didn't work. Newton felt as if they were attacking him, and he fought back.

One member of the Royal Society in particular made him very angry. This was a man named Robert Hooke. His job was to demonstrate experiments at the society's meetings. Hooke actually agreed with much of what Newton said. But he didn't believe that Newton's experiments really proved what Newton said they did.

Disagreement of this kind is common among scientists—it's an important way to work out the problems with an idea and to make new discoveries. Unfortunately, both Hooke and Newton were very sensitive and proud. They didn't just discuss ideas—they had fights. As the arguments grew worse, they insulted each other, and each accused the other of stealing ideas. They became enemies for life.

Newton never learned to enjoy give-and-take arguments with his fellow scholars. He missed working alone, entirely for his own satisfaction. "I desire to decline being involved in such troublesome & insignificant Disputes," he proclaimed. He went back to working all by himself.

Chapter 7

A Secret Life

Arguing with other scholars was not Newton's only problem. He also had a more personal difficulty. Newton was a fellow of Cambridge University. Being a fellow meant the university gave him money to live and work there, safe from the world outside. Cambridge was part of the Church of England. Every fellow had to become a minister in the church within seven years. By 1674, Newton's seven years were almost up. But he couldn't become a minister because, secretly, he didn't accept the teachings of the church.

Newton was a Christian and very serious about his religion. However, being Newton, he wasn't willing to just accept someone else's explanation about anything important.

Newton read the Bible with the same fierce, questioning mind he turned on the natural world. He decided that he did not agree with the Church of England about the Holy Trinity. The church said that God was one being, made up of the Father, the Son, and the Holy Ghost, and all three were divine. To stay at Cambridge, Newton would have to swear that he accepted this idea. But he didn't—he thought it was wrong to call Christ God. If he refused to agree with what the church said, he would be forced to leave Cambridge in disgrace, but he didn't want to lie about something so important.

In 1675, he approached King Charles II. He thought the king might be able to help him because he was the head of the Church of England. Newton didn't want to tell the king the real reason for his problem. Instead he explained that he wasn't just a fellow of the university. He was also a professor of mathematics. According to Newton, this meant he should not have to become a minister. This argument didn't really make sense. Fortunately, King Charles didn't care. Newton didn't have to become a minister, the king decided. He was able to stay at Cambridge without having to lie.

Just as he had a secret religious life, Newton also had a secret scientific life. He wanted to unlock the mysteries of alchemy. Alchemy was part magic, part religion, and part science. In secret, alchemists searched for the Philosopher's Stone, which would turn other metals into gold, and the Elixir of Life, which would grant immortality.

Newton spent even more time and energy on alchemy than he did on ordinary science. His servant reported that Newton often sat up all night in his private lab at Cambridge, bent over a roaring fire, working on mysterious experiments.

This might seem odd and puzzling. Why was a scientist involved with secret rituals and magic? Actually, it's not hard to guess why alchemy might appeal to him. He hated to have his work criticized in public. Alchemy offered him a perfect excuse to keep it secret. Alchemists considered themselves special, much wiser than ordinary people. Newton liked seeing himself as part of this select group.

But there was more to Newton's interest than that. In Newton's time, science was still in an early stage. It was not always possible to separate myths from facts. Alchemists believed they could turn other metals into gold because they thought that everything was made up of tiny particles that could be separated and recombined to make something else.

The questions the alchemists asked were not foolish. Some of their knowledge would eventually lead to modern chemistry and contribute to our knowledge of how atoms combine to form molecules.

Still, this was the Age of Enlightenment. Serious thinkers were turning away from the idea of special, secret wisdom available only to the chosen few. After Newton died, the Royal Society discovered he had written over a million words about alchemy. They were so embarrassed by this that they marked the papers "not fit to be printed." Newton's writings about alchemy were not published until 2004.

Chapter 8

A Competition

After his fight with the Royal Society, Newton withdrew into himself. He concentrated on his secret study of alchemy. He claimed he wasn't interested in scientific research anymore. Maybe he meant what he said at the time, but his greatest work was still ahead of him.

In 1684, three members of the Royal Society were chatting in a coffeehouse about current scientific issues. These three were Newton's enemy Hooke, a young astronomer named Edmond Halley, and Christopher Wren, a famous architect. Wren had been trying to understand how and why planets orbited the sun. Now he asked the other two men for help.

People already knew what path an orbiting planet actually followed. Johannes Kepler had shown in 1609 that it was an ellipse. They also knew that the amount of force between the planet and the sun decided the path of the orbit. But something else was involved that no one could figure out. The strength of the force changed in a complicated way, depending on how far apart the two bodies were. The force got weaker as the planet and the sun got farther apart. That made sense, but the force and the distance didn't seem to change at the same rate. The force changed faster and faster the more the distance grew. No one could figure out exactly what the relationship between the distance and the force was.

Scholars had come up with various ideas to explain the relationship. One suggestion was a mathematical relationship called the inverse square rule. Wren thought this might be the right one, but he had tried to prove it, and he couldn't.

Wren put the problem to his friends. Could they prove—using mathematics—that the inverse square rule would produce an elliptical orbit? If so, they would have created an important new law about the way the planets moved.

Hooke bragged that he had already done this, but he wasn't ready to tell the others how. First he wanted them to try and fail. Then he would show them. Wren and Halley didn't take Hooke very seriously. (When Newton had produced his wonderful telescope, Hooke claimed that *he* had already made a telescope that worked even better and was so small he could hang it from his watch chain.) Wren offered a prize—a valuable book—to whoever could show him the mathematical proof first.

After two months, Hooke still hadn't shown him anything. Nervously, Halley decided to approach the prickly Newton. Like Hooke, Newton said he had already proved that the inverse square rule would produce an elliptical orbit, years before. Unfortunately he wasn't sure where he had put the proof. He had only done it for his own amusement. He promised to send it to Halley as soon as he found it. Unlike

Hooke, Newton wasn't just bragging. Within a few months, Newton was able to send Halley his proof.

Halley's Comet

A comet is a bright object like a star in the sky, often with a long tail. In Newton's time, people believed comets were signs from heaven that something terrible (or wonderful) was going to happen. In 1682, a bright comet appeared. Newton's friend Edmond Halley read old reports from astronomers going back for many years. He noticed that there were reports of some kind of bright object appearing in the sky just about every seventy-six years. He made a brilliant leap and guessed that it was actually the same comet coming back over and over. This would mean comets orbited the sun, just like the planets—only comets had a much longer orbit. He predicted that it would appear again in 1758. Halley was already dead by then, but when the comet reappeared just as he said it would, it was named in his honor.

Chapter 9

Newton's Big Book

Halley's question rekindled Newton's interest in the way planets moved. He wrote a nine-page essay to answer it and then kept on going. "Now that I am upon this subject," he wrote, "I would gladly know the bottom of it." In only eighteen months, he finished his five-hundred-page masterpiece. The title is *Mathematical Principles of Natural Philosophy*, familiarly known from its Latin title as *Principia*. With this book, he laid the foundation of modern physics. Every physicist since 1687 has built their work on the ideas in Newton's book.

Halley was excited. He wanted to make sure Newton didn't keep this revolutionary work to himself. He acted as

Newton's editor and even paid for the book to be printed.

Right away, it looked as if there might be trouble. Newton's old enemy, Hooke, claimed that Newton had taken ideas from him. Newton was so furious that he threatened not to publish at all. It took all Halley's tact to calm him down.

The book came out in 1687 and caused a sensation. Readers felt as if the universe had suddenly been explained to them. A French mathematician wondered, "Does Mr. Newton eat, drink, and sleep like other men?" (As we know, the answer to this was actually *no*.)

Probably the book was admired and discussed more than it was actually read. It was almost impossible to follow. Newton even hinted that he had done this deliberately. It was a way to protect himself from people asking stupid questions.

Newton's book made him so famous that he was elected to Parliament. He became a member of the government just in time to vote in favor of the Glorious Revolution of 1689. Except for this one important vote, which brought a new king to the throne of England, he did not take any active role in Parliament. The only time he actually spoke was to ask for a window to be closed.

Chapter 10

Laws of Motion

Over three hundred years after Newton's book was written, it is hard to understand how great its impact has been. The things he figured out now seem natural and obvious to us. This is because Newton completely changed the way people think. Today, even people who have never heard of Newton think of movement in the terms he invented.

What exactly was in his revolutionary book? The idea of gravity, to start with. Earlier, Newton had studied two forces. The first was the one that pulled the apple and the moon toward the Earth. The second was the one that made planets orbit the sun. He realized that these were both the same force. He gave it the name we still use today: "It is now established that this force is gravity, and therefore we shall call it gravity from now on."

Newton also created his three laws of motion. He had learned the first law from Galileo. It says that if something is moving, it will keep moving until something makes it stop. If something is sitting still, it won't move until some force makes it move.

The second law shows how much force is needed to make something move or stop moving.

The final law says that, "For every action there is an equal and opposite reaction." This means that every time you push on something, it pushes back just as strongly, but in the opposite direction.

If you're standing on a skateboard and you push against the ground, the ground pushes back against you, which is why the skateboard moves forward. Or think of a balloon filled with air. If you let go of the neck of the balloon, the air rushes out of the balloon backward.

This pushes the balloon forward with the same force, so the balloon flies through the air. This same principle makes a rocket's engine work.

Newton's three laws explain the movement of everything in the universe. When combined with a lot of mathematics, these laws can predict everything from tides on Earth to the movement of stars in distant galaxies.

One odd thing is missing from Newton's explanation of gravity. Although he described how gravity acts, he never said exactly what it is. We can't blame him for this—three hundred years later, we still don't really know.

Chapter 11

Becoming a Legend

After his book came out, Newton became legendary. Suddenly Cambridge students saw him in a whole new way. "We gaz'd on him . . . as on someone divine," one recalled.

His life, however, continued more or less unchanged for the next few years. Then in 1693, Newton had a mental breakdown. He couldn't eat or sleep. He wrote his friends strange letters saying he wished they were dead. He accused them of trying to get him in trouble with women.

When he recovered, he decided he needed a change. In 1696, he asked some powerful friends to help him find a new job. They arranged for him to help run the Royal Mint.

The Mint was the place that created all England's

coins. It was in the Tower of London. Newton moved into a grand house in London. His friends expected he would hire someone else to do most of the work. Instead, Newton threw himself into the job.

For years, counterfeiters had been clipping bits of silver off the edges of coins to make new coins. By Newton's time, much of England's money was worth less than it was supposed to be. The government had to do something. They decided on the Great Recoinage of 1696.

The Mint collected all the clipped coins and remade them into a new form of coin. These coins had ridged edges, so they were harder to fake. Newton oversaw the whole thing. He did such a good job that in 1699 he was promoted to Master of the Mint. He stayed in this position for almost thirty years, until he died.

Once the Great Recoinage was done, Newton turned his attention to catching counterfeiters. He made himself into a kind of detective with a network of spies and informers. His greatest triumph was the capture of the clever counterfeiter named Chaloner. Newton pursued him for years and finally succeeded in having him executed.

During his first few years in London, Newton kept his distance from the Royal Society. He didn't want any more fights. In 1703, his old enemy Hooke died. The president of the society died the same year. Newton was immediately elected in his place. In 1704, Newton finally published his theory of optics. The book was based on research from many years earlier, but as he explained, "To avoid being engaged in Disputes about these matters, I have hitherto delayed the printing." He meant that he had waited until Hooke was dead.

Chapter 12

Battles at the Royal Society

Newton ruled the Royal Society like a tyrant. This led to some ugly incidents. The worst was the fight about who really invented calculus. Newton had created his form of calculus, the method of fluxions, as early as 1665, but he had refused to publish it. Only a few carefully chosen people got the chance to see it.

Around 1675, a German mathematician named Gottfried Leibniz had come up with a similar system, which he called calculus. It isn't surprising that someone else would make the same discovery as Newton had. After all, Leibniz had been working on the same kinds of problems. He had even written to Newton about his new kind of mathematics. (Ironically, he began one letter, "How great I think the debt owed you . . .") Leibniz published his paper on calculus in 1684.

At first, there didn't seem to be a problem. Then in 1704, Newton finally published his version of calculus. An anonymous reviewer hinted that he might have borrowed some of Leibniz's ideas.

Newton was furious. He didn't want anyone else to get the credit for inventing calculus. An ugly battle began, with Newton accusing Leibniz of stealing ideas from him. At first Leibniz was reasonable. "Mr. Newton developed it further, but I arrived at it by another way," he wrote to a friend. "One man makes one contribution, another man another."

Newton didn't think this made any difference. "Second inventors," he claimed, "have no right."

Finally in 1711, Leibniz appealed to the Royal Society to settle the fight, but Newton was president of the society. He put himself in charge of the committee looking into the issue. What's more, he secretly wrote the committee's report himself.

Published in 1713, the report twisted the evidence to make it seem that Leibniz had stolen Newton's work. Leibniz died three years later. Newton never regretted what he had done. Years later, he recalled happily that he "had broke Leibniz's Heart."

In one sense, however, Leibniz won the calculus wars. Newton's method of fluxions was a kind of personal shorthand. He never meant it to be used by anyone else. Leibniz's system was easier for other people to understand. Everyone who learns calculus today uses Leibniz's terms, symbols, and methods, not Newton's. Even the name *calculus* is from Leibniz. If Newton knew, he would be furious.

Chapter 13

Genius

Despite being so frail as a baby, Newton lived to be an old man. By his last years he was wealthy, powerful, and respected. In 1705, he was knighted by Queen Anne. He became Sir Isaac Newton.

Newton's mind remained sharp and his health mostly good almost to the end. He led a meeting of the Royal Society less than a month before his death.

He died on March 20, 1727, at age eighty-five. He was buried in London's Westminster Abbey—the first scientist to receive such an honor. The inscription on his fancy marble monument shows what awe he inspired. "Here is buried Isaac Newton, Knight, who by a strength of mind almost divine . . .

explored . . . what no other scholar has previously imagined." The great poet Alexander Pope wrote of him: "Nature and Nature's Laws lay hid in Night. God said, 'Let Newton be!' and all was light."

A mind almost divine—this is a grand claim. Still, scientists from Newton' s time through our own agree. What Newton accomplished was greater than his individual discoveries. He wanted to understand how everything fit together. It was as if other scholars had written interesting sentences, but Newton figured out the way all these sentences could be put together to tell the story of how the universe worked.

Newton knew that he had only begun to tell this story. As an old man he said, "I don't know what I may seem to the world, but as to myself, I seem to have been only like a boy playing on the sea-shore and diverting myself in now and then finding a smoother pebble or a prettier shell than ordinary, whilst the great ocean of truth lay all undiscovered

Westminster Abbey

Restoration of Westminster Abbey began in the year 1245. Kings, queens, and their families are usually married and crowned there. Until the 1760s, it was also where most of them were buried. People who worked for the church were also buried there. Starting around the time Newton was a child, being buried in Westminster Abbey became a way to honor someone for special achievements. Great generals, politicians, poets, and musicians were recognized in this way. Isaac Newton was the first scientist.

before me."

For the next two hundred years, almost all physics had its roots in his ideas. Only at the beginning of the twentieth century did another great genius— Albert Einstein—discover the limits of Newton's discoveries. In day-to-day life, however, people rarely have to deal with situations where Newton's physics doesn't make sense. It's still the way we understand the world. Whether we are riding a bicycle, catching a baseball, or dropping an apple, most of us most think of movement in terms we learned from that strange, bad-tempered, brilliant loner Isaac Newton.

Timeline of Isaac Newton's Life

1642	Isaac Newton is born on December 25.
1654	Moves to a nearby town to attend grammar school.
1661	Enters Trinity College, Cambridge.
1665	Graduates from Cambridge with a BA.
	Moves back to his mother's farm to escape the plague.
1668	Receives his master's degree from Cambridge.
1669	Becomes Lucasian Professor of Mathematics.
1671	Sends his reflecting telescope to the Royal Society.
1672	Elected to the Royal Society.
1679	Newton's mother, Hannah, dies.
1684	Halley, Hooke, and Wren meet at a coffeehouse to discuss planetary motion.
1687	Newton's *Principia* published.
1689	Elected to Parliament.
1693	Suffers a nervous breakdown.
1696	Moves to London to work at the Mint.
1699	Appointed Master of the Mint.
1703	Elected President of the Royal Society.
1704	Publishes his research on optics.
1705	Knighted.
1712	The Royal Society establishes a committee to decide who invented calculus.
1727	Isaac Newton dies, March 20.

Timeline of the World

1642	Civil war breaks out in England.
1648	The Thirty Years' War ends in Europe.
1649	King Charles I beheaded, January 30.
1660	Charles II restored as king of England.
	Royal Society founded.
1663	Robert Hooke invents the word "cell" to describe what he sees in the microscope.
1665	Plague breaks out in England.
1666	Great Fire of London.
1667	Milton publishes *Paradise Lost.*
1670	Charleston (originally called Charles Towne) is founded in North America by the British.
1675	Pocket watch invented.
1682	Halley's comet appears.
1688—1689	Glorious Revolution in England.
1689	A bill of rights guarantees Englishmen some freedom of speech and religion.
1692	The Salem witch trials take place in Massachusetts.
1694	The Bank of England is established.
1706	Benjamin Franklin is born.
1709	The "Great Frost" is the coldest winter in Europe in over five hundred years.
1712	First practical steam engine built.
1727	Janet Horne becomes the last person in Britain to be executed as a witch.

Bibliography

Ackroyd, Peter. Newton. New York: Doubleday, 2006.

*Christianson, Gale E. Isaac Newton and the Scientific Revolution. New York: Oxford University Press, 1996.

Gleick, James. Isaac Newton. New York: Pantheon Books, 2003.

*Krull, Kathleen. Giants of Science: Isaac Newton. New York: Viking, 2006.

Westfall, Richard S. The Life of Isaac Newton. New York: Cambridge University Press, 1993.

*Books for young readers